www.finishinglinepress.com

Womb Worlds

poems by

Lisa Molina

Finishing Line Press
Georgetown, Kentucky

"There are many events
in the womb of time,
which will be delivered."
~William Shakespeare~

Womb Worlds

To
Thomas, for giving me permission to share your story,
and for inspiring me daily with your strength and tenacity.

And
Gary and Bella, for all we have been through together.
Thank you for still dancing with me.
*** *

And
Eternal Gratitude
To the forever-unknown couple,
who donated your child's umbilical cord blood cells,
so that my child could live.

ACKNOWLEDGMENTS

Thank you to these journals, in which these poems first appeared, sometimes
in slightly modified versions:

Amethyst Review: "Waiting for Life" and "Washing My Feet" and "Trance"
Ancient Paths Literary Magazine: "When We Held Hands"
Eris & Eros Review: "World Womb"
The Peeking Cat 2021 Anthology: "Saved"
The Poet Magazine Christmas Anthology 2020: "Christmas of Lights"
Quillkeepers Press: Tan Lines Summer Anthology: "Helios Will Return"
Silver Birch Poetry and Press: "Back to the Womb," (originally "How to Go
Back to Paradise")
Sledgehammer Literary Journal: "Life Still Dances" and "Each Time"
Tiny Seed Literary Journal: "Anxious Autumn Leaves" and "Blizzard"
Trouvaille Review: "Emerging" and "Prognosis Percentage"
Wild Greens Magazine: "Fragments" (originally published as "Stardust.")

Fahmidan Publishing & Co: "Don't Fall in Love with Sisyphus," Digital
chapbook, February 2022, in which the following poems appear: "Back to
the Womb," "Christmas of Lights," "Helios will Return," "Life Still Dances,"
"No Words," "Prognosis Percentage," "Saved," "Trance," "Waiting for Life,"
"When We Held Hands," "World Womb."

Publisher: Leah Huete de Maines
Editor: Christen Kincaid
Cover Art: Kim Eitze
Interior Art: Kim Eitze - Tunnel; Lotus
And Ryan Logan: Life Still Dances - Watercolor
Author Photo: I.R. Molina
Cover Design: Elizabeth Maines McCleavy

Order online: www.finishinglinepress.com
also available on amazon.com

Author inquiries and mail orders:
Finishing Line Press
PO Box 1626
Georgetown, Kentucky 40324
USA

Table of Contents

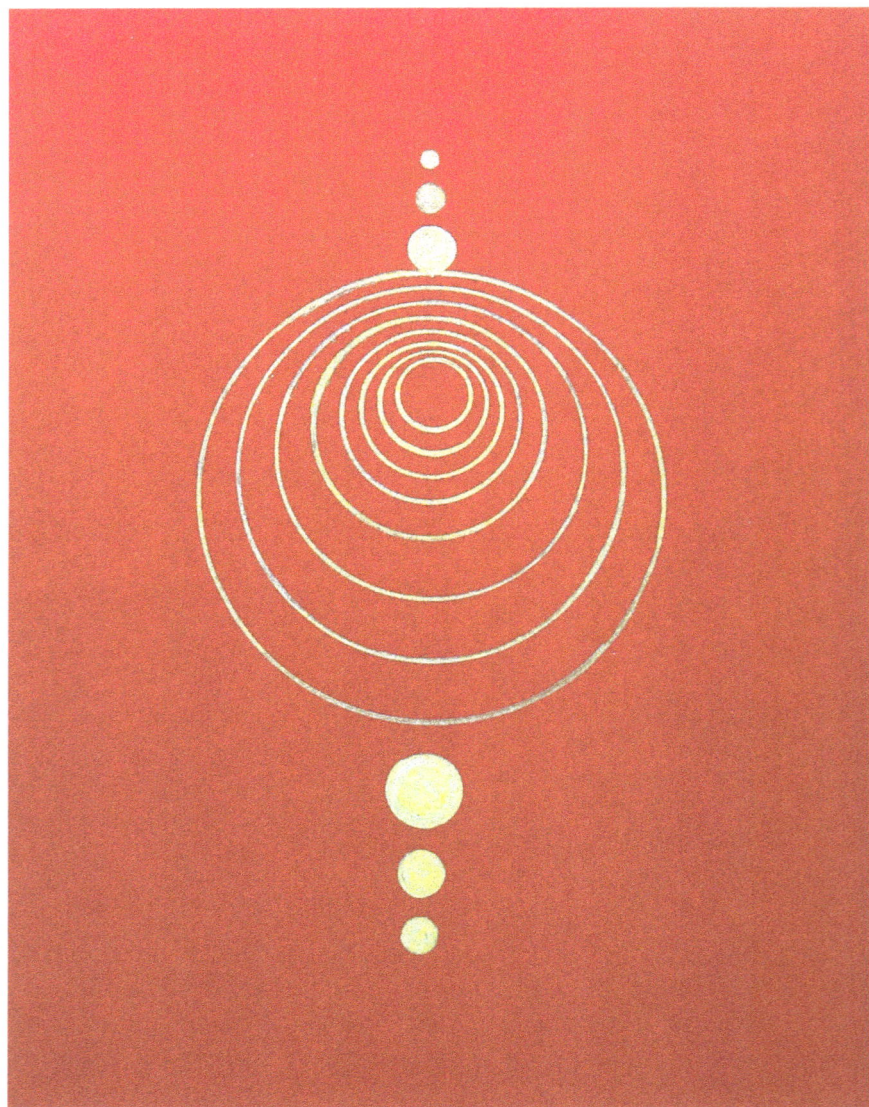

Emerging

How to reach the center?

Holding together this universe,
that by some law of physics
is pulling itself apart
with no center of gravity.

What do the swirling,
seemingly out of control
events of life-

The kaleidoscope of
people, memories,
fear of future,
and numbness require
in order to be
planted, nurtured, grounded?

There is a liminal space;
A gift of ribbon-wrapped presence
that I so carefully open.

The gift is
time, trials,
and testimonials
of teachers, gurus.

Only then will I
experience the
Alchemy,
transforming the womb's darkness
to golden light.

Fragments

Pinpoints of life-
fragments of
exploding stars.

Moon eggs float
contentedly in a
mother's womb

Growing, stretching, turning,
hearing the rhythm of
the heart blood flowing.

Seeking more space
pushing and prodding
to discover new worlds

even if by pain,
blood, fear, and
saltwater tears.

Still connected by
the stardust within all
of Mother Earth,

and the rhythm
of life waves
breathing,

In and Out
Back and Forth
Ebbing and Flowing

Whoosh Whoosh Whoosh

Wet Warm Waves

Whoosh Whoosh Whoosh

Life bathing in the waters
floating freely as heart
pulsating blood pumping
the world of the womb.

The life waters soon gushing
forth into the world of air
and waves of babes suckling
their mothers' breasts.

Now waves of
belly breath;
Rising falling
Rising falling

Waves on life's shores;
Despair Hope
Anguish Joy
Horror Ecstasy

Coming
Receding
Coming
Receding

Life, death
Life, death

New life forming
floating freely in

Wet Warm
Womb Waves.

Question for Mary

Did you know when you
carried your son in your womb,
anxiously and excitedly awaiting
his emergence into this world,
the suffering he would
eventually endure?

I don't know.

I do believe that you, like me,
rubbed your swollen belly,
felt joy at the first fluttering
of movement, and spoke
tenderly to the baby in your
womb living within you.

Waiting patiently,
for his humble
and glorious birth.

I do know that I thought of you often
as I watched in agony my son suffering
the horrors of cancer.

Body
slowly
dying.

And I envisioned both of us,
as we helplessly bore witness,
pleading with and begging to God,

"Take me instead!"

Blizzard

Winds howling;
calling my name.

Forcing myself out;

Steeling myself
against sharp ice
cutting slicing
ears, eyes, hair.

Digging, clawing
the frozen earth;
Hands bleed.
White snow ice
transforms to
embryonic pink.

Hiding, residing
underground,

Waiting.

Will I suck all the air
from this atmosphere?

My flesh feeding
worms, ants,
and roots of trees?

Holding breath.
Listening for signs.
Silence. Sleep.

The ice
drips
drips
drips

Until
out of this
world womb
I fly.

Christmas of Lights
~For our dear friends

'Twas the night before Christmas...

Our three-year-old cancer-fighter
in Superman pajamas, hanging
on to life by a thread.

Will it hold?

Untethered from IV pumps
on the pediatric cancer floor,
allowed to go home one night only:

Christmas Eve.

"His last?"
We ask ourselves silently.

Snakelike-tube still protruding
from his chest, so I may connect
the IV bag hanging over his bed,

Will he dream of sugarplums
dancing in his now bald head?

Wishing Santa will bring more
trains for his set, and perhaps
superheroes- Batman, Superman-?

While Saint Nick is packing his sleigh
full of toys, we pack up our car
full of medical supplies.

A small Christmas tree awaits
in the house, and stockings we
hung on the fireplace with care,

With hopes that
good blood counts
soon would be there.

When turning the
corner to our home,
what do I see?
A hallucination?
From sleep deprivation?

My lips lift to a smile,
while warm, salty tears
blur the vision of my eyes;

My husband laughing,
giggling, says to our son,
"Look, Andrew, look!"

I turn to look as his
puffy eyes open.

Disoriented by drugs,
his voice whispers,

"Home."

We stop,
to gawk,

and gaze,
amazed.

White
Bright
Light

illuminates the
long-barren home.

Glimmering.
Glowing.
Despair lifting,

Going.

We get out of the car
and stand on the
grass.

Husband holding our son
tightly to his chest,
Our faces reflecting the
bright gleaming light.
Clear air cool.
Stars twinkling overhead.

Our first cancer-Christmas
with the child of my womb,

miraculously, now
breaks through the gloom

by the simple act of friends:
House shining under moon.

Now hope firmly held and
bathed in pure white.

I look to the stars dangling,
tiny sparkles in the night.

And once again,
Believe.

Life Still Dances
~For Gary

We're in the pediatric cancer unit.

Liquid chemo dripping through
the snake-like tube pressed
into your chest,

Leading to your heart, destroying
all the cancer cells in your
puffed swollen body.

But it's Mardi Gras!

Your dad comes into the
hospital room carrying
a loaded box full
of hope.

Of normalcy.

We put on the beads.
We play the zydeco music.

We devour the purple green gold
king cake with the baby inside its
womb of wheat, sugar, and eggs.

We help you out of the bed, IV pole
still attached to the tube in your chest,
as a cord once attached you to my womb.

Your little sister reaches for your hands.

The music louder.
The sounds of accordion,
singing, rhythms thumping.

You move together.
Swaying
Smiling

Dancing
Laughing.

I'm dancing in reverie with your father.

The nurses come in,
clapping laughing.

It is a dance of
the exquisite
Normal

nearly lost
in our lives,

that cancer cannot
take away from us.

Hope always
moves and grooves
to the dance of life.

So
Dance!
Life!
Dance!

Prognosis Percentage

The boy, age thirteen,
battling leukemia 3 times since he was three,
asks the transplant doctor,
"What are my chances of surviving, Dr. Lee?"

Dr. Lee locks eyes with boy, intentionally,
and says,
"40%."
Somewhat confidently.

Furiously, insistently,
boy pounds fist on table
"I'll take nothing less than 50!"
Negotiating for his life, desperately.

A roar of silence.
Air is hot.
The agonizing 3-second wait.

Doctor Lee's eyes crinkle as he laughs,
offering out his hand, the boy's to grasp.

"You've got it!" he says.

The deal is done.
The bidding won.
All parties agree.
Heartily.

And that boy-fighter
of unrelenting hope,
Is given 10 percent more,
So that he may cope.

Prognosis percentage?
It's just a number to hear.

For no quantification can suffice,
The value of my womb child's life.

Trance

Moon shaped as a C
C for cancer
C for chance
C for cure

The nurses hang
the bags of potions
casting the killing spells
on all his blood cells.

My ritual now;
light an electric candle,
brew some herbal tea,
listen to the
whooshing
whishing
(wishing)
of the
cat-purring
pumps.

Pulsating pumping
in this room of
nearly-broken hearts.

Lying on the bed
across the room
from my sleeping son,

I squeeze
each separate
bead-bead-bead
of my Rosary;

"And blessed is the
fruit of thy womb..."

"And blessed is the
fruit of thy womb..."

Until I drift
into the trance
of night.

I awaken to
swishing
(wishing)
sounds
of the janitor
sweeping.

Morning sun conjures
a beam of golden light
onto his placid pale
puffy face-

An angel's charm.

For today, the
umbilical cord cells
of another mother's
womb-child will
resurrect his
blood.

The supernatural bond
between these children
never to be broken.

Stepping out of bed,
I walk to the mirror over
the sanitized sink, where

the unrecognizable
frightened face
gazes back at me,
and asks herself,

"Is this real?"

Saltless Tears

I have cried so much,
I have no salt left.
Even though my oceanic body

is full of its flavorful taste,
my tears just come and come,
rising in waves so high,

the salt is left underneath
to season the undertow
of feelings that push and pull.

My saltless tears become
tidal waves of sadness.
Will the salt ever

rise from the depths
to comfort me by
infusing my tears

with it, and
return them to
oneness with the

universal
womb
sea?

Waiting for Life

I am still waiting

in the pediatric
cancer transplant
unit.

Ten days
and nights.
So far.

Will his body embrace
the donated cord
blood cells?

(As my womb once
embraced him as an
unborn child?)

Or reject them.
Refuse them.
Causing his death.

The children
on the other sides
of two walls

of our room
have whispered
their final breaths.

My child is still breathing.
Living a life
between deaths.

What is he dreaming?
Has he descended to the depths?
Lying in a dark womb cave?

Lazarus awaiting?

Saved

Pink pulsating
womb cord
joins
mother daughter
together.

At birth,
extra cord cells
collected,
frozen,

Saved.

Graciously given
to
unknown
boy's
cancer-ridden
body.

Eleven years later,
boy is now
pulsating with
fresh pink
pure blood.

The boy
and girl
bound together
by the
shared cord
and blood
of Life.

For eternity.
Anonymously.

Saved.

Listening

I still hear the
constant, soothing
churning

Of waves rolling
 on a beach;

Or the womb
 of my mother;

Or the womb
  of the mother

who gave her
  baby's cord blood

to save the
  life of mine.

Looking out the window,
I see bright mother moon
directing the flowing tides,

and smile
in gratitude,
as I listen;

Whoosh
Whoosh
Whoosh

Waiting to Remember

Placing the coffee cup that counts my days
into the dishwasher, I remember
I need to pay a bill upstairs.

I turn on the dishwasher.

Oh, how I love the
whoosh, whoosh, whoosh
sound of it.

Music of the pumping
mother's womb.
The primal pulse of life.

Am I somehow still yearning for that
safe, warm, wet whoosh where I can
be nourished, floating, growing?

No wondering if there was anything
I could have done to prevent my child
from getting cancer again and again?

No guilt for the mothers and fathers
whose children died of cancer even
as mine survived against all odds?

Whoosh whoosh whoosh…

My cell phone buzzes.

I open my eyes and I'm upstairs in my bedroom.
(How did I even get here?)

I hear the churning dishwasher.

What did I come upstairs for?

I stand alone, just waiting
to remember what it is
I forgot.

Anxious Autumn Leaves

Anxious autumn leaves
Wind through trees
Blowing howling
Shrieking tearing
Violently ripped
From their branches.

Spinning wildly
Soaring spiraling
Up and around
Until until until
Falling
Falling
Falling
To their deaths.

The naked trees can only
Watch.
And wait.
For the winter rest.

Silence.

Internal strength building
For a new Spring.

My anxious soul
That has also blown wildly
Often becoming untethered
From its branches.

Falling
Falling
Falling.
Now, finally,
Heeds the voices
Of the leaves
And trees.

Embracing their wisdom;
The nourishment of
A winter's rest;
Building strength for
A gleaming, glistening
Rebirth from the fertile
Womb of Spring.

My leaves will grow
And give birth
Once more
To Hope.

Washing My Feet
~For Bella

Your tiny toes waved at us
through the ultrasound monitor.

A few years later
in the twilight of evening,
when I was cleaning you in the
womb-like water of a bath,
I dipped my cold feet in
to warm them.

You gently took one into
your hands and began to wash
my dirty, stinky, tired, old feet.
Washing them clean from the
journeys of the day.

This soon became our nightly ritual:

Baptisms through simple acts of love.

A loving mother's care washing
her child's silky black hair.

A child's soft and innocent touch,
refreshing her tired mother's feet;

And soul-

You're a young woman now.
I sometimes watch your bare toes wiggle
as you lie on the couch reading a book.

Sometimes they wave to me;
Unknowingly.

And I wiggle mine;
Remembering;
Gratefully.

My soul once again,
Refreshed.

Each Time

Each time your lips
are pale like snow

Each time you complain
of aching bones

Each time you sleep
for hours a day

Each time a cold
won't go away

———————————

Each time red blood
drips from your nose

Each time a purple
bruise that grows

Each time, three, much
worse than before

Each time you cried,
"No more! No more!"

———————————

Each time like these
flash memories

Each time the womb
of suffering

Each time a reminder
of strength and grace

Each time you
stared fear in the face.

World Womb

In the museum,
I turn the corner
from Vincent's Irises,

And gasping,
Georgia's World Womb facing me
-Shockingly-

God's hands embracing the universe,
while an open womb waits.

Creation of the infinite;
and the infinitesimal.

Oh! How I shriek and shake.

No Words

*"I found I could say things with colors and shapes that I couldn't
say any other way—things I had no words for."*
~Georgia O'Keeffe

You spoke to me through your colors
and shapes thirty-three years ago.
.
How could I have known when
I saw the poster hanging in the
shop window that you were
foretelling my future?

Me, a barely-breathing
statue standing frozen

in the middle of the mall,
viscerally reacting to
your pulsing womb
placenta of pastels;

Hands holding all of creation in infinity.

So began your vocal visions, whispering to
me through your mystical colors and shapes.

Twenty-one years later, that poster
still faithfully framed and hung,
freed my frantic fears,
when my womb's child,

whose blood was filled
with cancer, killing him,

was resurrected by the pulsating
purple pink poppy red cord blood
that once connected a forever-
unnamed child to her mother.

The cord of life tying us together forever, all.

Two years ago, you shocked me again,
 (Oh, how you must have laughed)

when I turned the corner from Vincent's irises and
there was your creation staring back at me. I had never
before experienced the real flesh and blood lines and
shapes so sensuously stroked by your soulful hands.

Shapes/shared/spaces/creating/undulating/in/out/in/out/crevices/clean/
clear/creations.

Lines are lives.
Curves are quests.

Colors are cosmic constellations bursting forth
lifelines to be lived in the ever-eternal ether.

Hands/holding/healing/heroic/hearts/heralding/home.

My living son,
with his unknown
twin sister
breathing,
as I gasp.

Weep.

You're right, Georgia.

There are
no words.

When We Held Hands

"You have your father's hands."
I said after your tiny waxy wet
body emerged from my womb,

Fingers thin and long.

Three years later, I held one of your
hands as you wailed at the shock of pain,
as a nurse pricked one of those fingers;

The blood soon revealing your body was full of leukemia cells.

I held your hands throughout the thirty-eight months
of chemotherapy, clumps of your hair falling into my
hands as I would wash it, until none was left.

I felt those tiny hands as fists banging on my chest
because you were so furious that this "medicine" that
was going to make you well made you feel so sick.

I felt those hands squeezing mine
across the table eight years later
when the cancer returned.

"Mom, I don't want to die. Tell me I'm not going to die. Please! Tell me I
won't die."

I sat caressing your hand while four nurses and a doctor worked furiously
to revive you while you lay unconscious in septic shock, nearly dying,
remembering the day I first saw and held them through a blur of tears.

And I held those skeleton-like
hands two years later when the
cancer was now in your brain;

And the umbilical cord blood of an
unknown savior child was transplanted
into your withering, nearly-dead body,

Resurrecting you.

_____

You're twenty-four now,
free of the tight grip of cancer.
We haven't held hands in many years;

But I look at them often, hoping
you don't notice; And I smile softly
as I watch those beautiful,

long-fingered hands you
inherited from your father,
pulsate with movement and life.

And I can still feel them holding mine.

Helios Will Return

Azure water cools,
while the gulls and I
speak in secrets only
we can understand.

Soothing scent of
saltwater fills my lungs,
traveling through my
body's pulsating cells.

Infinite horizon, as Helios
pulls the orange pink sun
down through the
end of the world.

Bright white moon
peeks her head up
wishing Helios
a safe journey.

This is no world of mere mortals.
Luna's glow creates a
line of light skipping over
the dark aquatic glass.

If her glow is a reflection of the sun,
then does the light on the water
emanate from her or the sun?

Or is it neither?

Perhaps the light I see
shines up from below;
Or they both shine
towards one another.

Luna and I wait
in joyful hope
for the dawn of
a new day.

Helios will emerge with
Light, from the womb
at the end of the world.

Back to the Womb

"And as life began in the sea, so each of us begins his identical life in a miniature ocean within his mother's womb."
~Rachel Carson

Rhythmic pumping
whooshing womb wave
sounds crash upon the
darkening beach;

My toes sink slightly in soft sand;
White frothy foam washes up
and clings to my legs.

I look up to the tiny sparkling eyes,
winking at me through
the onyx cover above.

Are they watching me
sparkle, wink, and shine?

As we gaze on each other,
I begin to spin.

As I turn turn turn,
the water begins to rise.

Rising up my calves, knees, thighs.
up to my belly;

The scar that once connected
me to my mother's womb, and
the belly that held my own babies.

It rises up over my breasts
that fed them warm milk, and
my heart still pulsing with life.

Feeling the soothing water
surrounding my arms,
shoulders and neck;

Throwing my head back as joyous
laughter laughter laughter
bursts forth from my mouth.

The stars and I still
shining on each other, and
Luna smiling down on me.

Louder laughter as the
nourishing waters of Eden
slowly climb

up up up
until my head is
covered completely;

My hair caressing my
face and shoulders.

My feet lifting off
the floor of the Earth.

My soul smiles.
It knows it
is safe,

as it returns
to the depths
of Paradise.

I'm floating,
flying,
in the

Wet
World
Womb.

Additional Acknowledgments

The Georgia O'Keeffe painting referenced in the collection is: *Gray Lines with Black Blue and Yellow.*

I am so grateful to Dr. James Sharp, Dr. Sharon Lockhart, and the staff of the Children's Blood and Cancer Center of Dell Children's Hospital of Austin, and Dr. Chan and staff of Methodist Children's Hospital Cancer and Blood Center of San Antonio for saving my son's life.

All of our family and friends who supported us on this tumultuous journey.

All of those children and their families who have suffered and endured pediatric cancer, for sharing your lives and the precious lives of your children with me.

Two Sylvias Press, for the online poetry retreats in which some of these poems were born, along with the support of the participants.

Kim Eitze, for her joyous, creative spirit, and for allowing me to enhance my words with her beautiful art.

Ryan Logan, coach and art teacher at James Bowie High School, Austin, TX, for his watercolor, "Life Still Dances."

Michael Reeves, journalism teacher at Bowie High School, for his help in formatting photos.

Zulfikar Ghose, poet, novelist, and essayist, my creative writing professor at The University of Texas at Austin, and still my mentor, over thirty years later. Thank you, Sir Ghose, my old guru.

Contest Recognition:

The Ekphrastic Review:
Finalist in the "Fifty Shades of Blue Contest," for her Flash Fiction piece, "The Young Man in the Moon."

Beyond Words Magazine:
Winner of 250-Word Creative Writing Challenge - February 2021, and August 2021 issues.
Her poem "Spring to Spring" chosen as winner of photography/art response published in December 2021 issue.

Raconteur Literary Magazine:
6-Word Contest—3rd place

The Literatus Magazine:
Molina featured as 'Poet of the Week' for her poem "Thinking of Sylvia" on their Instagram page for National Poetry Month, April 2021

Lisa Molina is a writer and retired educator in Austin, Texas, where she earned a BFA at the University of Texas at Austin. She has taught high school English and Theatre Arts, and was named Teacher of the Year by the Lake Travis ISD Education Foundation in 1992. She also served as Associate Publisher of *Austin Family Magazine*. In 2000, Molina began working with students with special needs.

Her digital chapbook, *"Don't Fall in Love with Sisyphus,"* published by Fahmidan Publishing & Co., launched in February 2022.

Molina's poetry, creative nonfiction, and fiction can be found in numerous online and print publications, including *Beyond Words Magazine, Trouvaille Review, Sparked Literary Magazine, The Ekphrastic Review, Neologism Poetry Journal, Fahmidan Journal, Sky Island Journal, Flash Fiction Magazine, Epoch Press Autumn 2021 "Transitions" issue, Bright Flash Literary Review, Ancient Paths Literary Magazine, Amethyst Review, Tiny Seed Literary Journal, Wild Greens Magazine, Pop the Culture Pill*, several *Quillkeepers Press Anthologies, The Peeking Cat 2021 Annual Anthology*, and several Anthologies published by *The Poet*.

She lives in Austin, Texas with her husband, two adult children, and two cats.

Read more of her words at: lisalitgeek.wordpress.com,
Twitter: @lisabmolina1,
Instagram: @lisabookgeek

www.ingramcontent.com/pod-product-compliance
Lightning Source LLC
Chambersburg PA
CBHW050029090426
42734CB00021B/3475